Don't Work Stupid, Coach Yourself

40 Things Managers Won't Tell You

A Step by Step Guide to Coach Yourself

Coaching for Success Series

by Mark A. Baggesen

Title: Don't Work Stupid, Coach Yourself

Subtitle: 40 Things Managers Won't Tell You–A Step by Step Guide to Coach Yourself

Disclaimer and FTC Notice

Cover designed by Romana Bovan. Contact/Portfolio: 99designs.com/profiles/246674

ISBN: 9781091977136

Find Mark A. Baggesen at: https://coachyourselfbooks.com

Dedication

May you be more successful than you dreamed possible.

Table of Contents

Preface

"The biggest difference is in the leadership. It was better for us. We had more coaches and mentors to help us. A lot of the younger players today suffer from a lack of direction."

~ Isaiah Thomas

Today's Workplace

Everyone knows that college is great for mental development, but it doesn't prepare one for the workplace. The only way for you to gain the skills to succeed is by learning from others, reading and coaching yourself consistently until you are successful. This book will guide you through that progress and provide dozens of additional resources for your development and reference.

The workplace differs greatly from 30 years ago. With the elimination of middle management in Corporate America, employees don't have the coaches or mentors that previous generations had available to them. They expect employees to do more with less because industry expected the computer to reduce work. In reality, it only reduced the number of workers–there is still a lot of work! Combine that and the lack of coaches and mentors and its easy to understand why employees today are at a huge disadvantage.

Coaches and Mentors

A coach or mentor is a trusted adviser or counselor. I have been one of those for about 25 years for people of diverse culture backgrounds from across the globe, those working face to face, those working remote, onshore and offshore for both professional and personal development.

- I have to imagine that if I were now in my 20s or 30s, I would ask these questions:

- How can I progress in my career and move to new levels of success with no road map?

- Other people have had great careers why aren't they sharing what they know and paying it forward?

- Why can't I get that promotion?

- Is this workplace all there is?

This book will save you from having to learn a lot of lessons the hard way. I say that because I will teach you how to coach yourself.

About Me and this Book

I have been in middle and senior management for the last 25 years for Fortune 500 companies. During that time, it has been my privilege to manage and mentor dozens of people. I am an expert at turning chaos into success, recovering failed technology projects and complex problem solving. My work is my play and I enjoy it.

I wrote this book because my time here is finite. Each year seems to pass faster than the last. The only way to multiply myself through others is with this book. This is my way to pay it forward. I hope to help many people and maybe even create legions of new coaches and mentors. The price of this book is very modest. I have done that with a purpose: I want to make it affordable to all.

If this book is helpful to you, maybe when you are successful and older, you will mentor deserving younger people, who will mentor others, who will mentor others. This will start a cycle of goodwill and knowledge that will outlive you, me and all those you help.

Preparation

Consider using a notebook to write your answers to all the questions in this book. It could be a composition book or a loose-leaf notebook. It doesn't matter. What matters is that you answer all questions honestly and fully. This is the only way that this book will be helpful for you.

You can read this book without a notebook. Long term though if you want to maximize this book's effectiveness for your career and life consider using a notebook.

I have a gift for you: A free collection of worksheets as well as a list of all online resources with hyperlinks mentioned in this book. The worksheets are available at coachyourselfbooks. com/worksheets/.

Print out the worksheet papers and use those as needed. Click on the resource links in the provided PDF file, to access dozens of other resources.

I recommend that you read this whole book through first (in a few days' time). Then go back and work through each chapter (in a few weeks). Allow yourself time and space to think about what you have read. Then answer the questions meaningfully. This is for you. You are worth the time!

Chapter 1: Where Have You Been?

"The Past is but the past of a beginning."

~ H. G. Wells

This chapter requires you to be brutally honest with yourself. It is important to take stock in what you have done and where you have been in the past. For each question, take a few minutes to think about the answer and write it down.

Questions to Ask Yourself

Start by asking yourself these questions:

- Am I now where I thought I would be 5 or 10 years ago?

- Am I where I wanted to be in my career and life?

If the answer is yes: Outstanding! Congratulations!

If the answer is no that's okay. But it's important to look at this. Ask yourself the following questions and write the answers:

- What did I want to be 5 or 10 years ago?

- What did I try to achieve that?

- Did I have a cohesive, well thought out plan? If, yes, what kept me from fulfilling that plan?

- Do I have any regrets about where I am in my life and career today?

- What would I do differently if I had the chance for a do-over?

The Past is the Past

The previous questions may evoke strong emotions in you. This is good! The purpose of this exercise isn't to "beat yourself up." The purpose is to give you insight into how fast life moves and that time waits for no one. That said, the past is the past and we can't do anything about it–it's done, finished, unchangeable, kaput, over. So, let it go. Your future will be fantastic!

Make a commitment to yourself right now. Commit 100% to making the next 10 years, a world of YOUR MAKING.

You can achieve all you want in your life and career. Begin by understanding that every day is a gift, and it is your decision how you use it. You can use it with purpose, or you can waste it and just let things happen. Once the day is over, it's over.

Commit to Yourself

Write this commitment statement (or one like it) on a blank piece of paper, sign and date it or use the free worksheet from the website. The worksheets are available at coachyourself-books.com/worksheets/.

Today, I totally commit to making the next 10 years, a future of MY MAKING.

I can do ANYTHING–I know that now.

I will use every day as if it were my last.

I understand that every new day is one more day than given to someone else.

I will create a plan for my future.

I will follow that plan so in 10 years, I will be where I want to be.

I will create my destiny!

Signed, <your name>   Today's Date is:

Put your signed statement on a wall or refrigerator–anywhere you will see it every day.

Summary

The past is the past, leave it there. This is your time. Use each day to its maximum.

Questions to Ask Yourself

- Have I taken the time to honestly and fully answer this chapter's questions?

- Am I able to let go of the past and move forward? If not, why not?

- Is there anything else that's now holding me back? If yes, what is it and what can I do about it?

Additional Resources

- PsychCentral.com – "Learning to Let Go of Past Hurts: 5 Ways to Move On"

- HuffPost.com – "When You're Living in the Past"

- BecomingMinimalist.com – "Don't Forget the Past. Learn from It."

- Psychology Today – "3 Definitions of Mindfulness That Might Surprise You"

- Headspace.com – an inexpensive service that uses a Smartphone app to help people maximize mindfulness, inner peace, and happiness.

Chapter 2: Coaching Yourself

If you believe in yourself and have dedication and pride and never quit, you'll be a winner. The price of victory is high but so are the rewards.

~ Bear Bryant

You Must Learn to Coach Yourself

What, I have to coach myself?

How the heck do I do that?

How do I know, what I don't know?

Often the only person you will depend on is yourself. From the time you leave the protection of your parents, until the end of your life, you have the power to be your best friend or worst enemy. What you think about yourself will have a lot to do with how successful you become in life.

Yes, there will be friends and colleagues along the way, but ultimately it is up to you to make your life and career what you want–no one will do that for you. Unless you are lucky enough to fall into a huge pile of money, you must build a career that can support you and your family to have the life you want and deserve.

Well-meaning friends sometimes will help you, but won't have the time or skills to be helpful. A former professor of mine from graduate school once said of colleagues: "Colleagues won't do much for you, anyway. But God help you if you make an enemy of one of them–they will spend the rest of their career trying to ruin yours." (Another reason to be nice to colleagues).

You should learn how to coach yourself. This book will show you how to do it. Once you are successful and on your path, if you can coach others and pay it forward, bonus–you will create a legacy.

Lesson 1: Carefully Choose Role Models

The first place to start is by observing and interacting with people around you. Specifically, people that are older, more mature or smarter than yourself. You can learn so much from surrounding yourself with people that are better or smarter than you at something–they will lift you up in ways you can't imagine!

For example, if you want to be a musician, surround yourself with musicians that are all better than you. You will learn a ton from them and you will become better. If you want to be a great manager, spend time with highly successful managers you know and reap the benefits of other people's knowledge and experience.

The alternative to choosing great people to surround yourself with is choosing people less than yourself. The problem with that is you probably won't learn much from them. They can bring you down with their problems, incorrect decisions, and behaviors. This is a huge activity trap and may be where the phrase "guilt by association" came from. It may not be a fair statement, but it is what it is. Unfortunately, little in life is fair.

In looking for friends and colleagues (at work, in social situations or in professional associations), choose people that are smarter, more successful and just seem to have the world under control in their lives and career. Choose people you think the world is a better place because they are in it. If you do this, you will learn new things at an incredible pace and it will change your life.

Look for skills or traits in people you admire and decide if you want to adopt any of those in your life. For example, if a teacher of yours is a gifted listener and can calm down even the most upset person, watch how they do it. Later, ask them for a few minutes of their time.

When you sit down with them, relate the situation or behavior you noticed them display. Ask them questions about how and where they learned how to do that. More than likely, they will be happy to share their opinions and ideas with you. Ask them about any books or articles on the subject they think might be helpful.

After you speak with them, do a good follow-up by either reading suggested materials, or by doing your own research. Then practice and add that talent to your skill set.

Some human traits and skills are innate, meaning you are born with those. For people that learn skills at an early age those seem second nature. However, you will learn many traits and skills throughout your life. If no one in your life has told you this before, here's it is:

- You can DO anything in this world.

- You can BE anything in this world.

- The only limitations you will EVER have are the ones you place on yourself.

If you doubt that statement, then you may need a daily affirmation. Write those statements down and say those to yourself every day until you know and feel this is true. Put this in a place you will see it every day. (The statement is part of the free worksheets) The worksheets are available at coachyourselfbooks.com/worksheets/.

The best way to progress is to learn and adopt traits and skills from smart and talented people until you become the person you want to be.

Observe people you admire and notice:

- What do they have to say about a subject?

- How do they express themselves?

- What is their body language?

- What results from their actions?

- What situations do they take part in and which do they try to avoid?

Any trait or skill you think is good, adopt and make it your own. Any you think is bad, discard. You can do this for your entire career and life. This process is just careful observation, critical thinking and doing whatever work it takes to make it part of you.

Use the Library

One of the best sources of information are books; books at the library. Libraries are full of all the information in the world that can make you successful.

Where to start, you ask?

Biographies and Autobiographies

Thousands of amazing people have lived before us. Times and situations change, but people are the same throughout generations. Read biographies and autobiographies about people you either admire or would like to better understand.

Seneca was a Roman Philosopher who lived in the first century AD. He had a brilliant mind and he wrote about a wide variety of topics. Although he died in 65 AD, his advice is as accurate and helpful today as it was 2000 years ago. How cool is that?

The great thing about biographies and autobiographies is that you can learn from the successes and failures of others, without having to go through those yourself. Yes, you will make mistakes in life, but you don't have the make the same mistakes other people have made!

George S. Patton

During World War II, one of most victorious leaders of the Allied Forces was George S. Patton. Would you like to guess why he was so successful?

The reason for Patton's success was that he carefully studied every battle ever fought (in known history) for each specific battlefield. Since his "theater of operation" was Europe, there were well-documented battles.

Patton learned the mistakes made, why the winners were victorious and all that was important. When he and his army went into combat, they had all the advantages learned from a thousand years of history.

Read biographies and autobiographies to absorb the wisdom and commit to memory, learned lessons relevant to you. You won't be disappointed.

Summary

- Coaching yourself will take real work, persistence, and resources.

- Choose your role models carefully. Adopt traits and skills that will make you the person you want to be. You can do this for both your personal life and career.

- Read biographies and autobiographies to learn from others.

Questions to Ask Yourself

- Who is someone I know that's smarter or better at something than I am?

- Would this person make a good role model for me?

- What skills and traits would I like to learn and adopt?

- (Ask these questions as many times as needed, to create a list of role models).

Additional Resources

- WikiHow Article–How to Choose a Role Model

- US News and World Reports-"6 Tips for Choosing a Good Role Model"

- US News and World Reports-"7 Types of Friends You Need to Break Up With"

- TutorialsPoint.com Article-"What You Can Learn from Biographies"

Chapter 3: The Right Questions

"The art and science of asking questions is the source of all knowledge."

~ Thomas Berger

Lesson 2: Ask the Right Questions

Life, career, relationships, problems, everything is about asking the right questions. You need not know everything, but you need to be able to find everything.

The way to find everything is by asking the right questions. You should learn how to ask about the right thing, at the right time, to the right people.

How many times in your life have you wished you had asked more of the right questions before deciding?

Some Questions are Tougher than Others

Years ago, Bob sat across from an employee on his first day of work. He was new to the company and wanted to get to know all the employees he had just been given to manage. He started with these questions: "Where do you want to be in your career in 10 years? What would you like to be doing?" There was a dead silence, and a puzzled look on the employee's face. After about 10 seconds, he said "Ah,... I don't know."

The second, third and fourth person gave Bob a similar answer. The fifth person said, "I'd like to be a manager someday." Eighty percent of his employees had no idea where they wanted to be in their career or what they wanted to do in 10 years. (These people had already been in their careers for 5 to 15 years).

Have you asked yourself this question yet? Where do I want to be in my career in 10 years? If so, write your answer down as a statement in your notebook:

"In 10 years, I want to be <where>, doing <what>."

If you don't have an answer that's okay. Most people don't know what they want or where they want to be in 10 years—this concept just seems too far away for most people to consider. In reality, 10 years is right around the corner and when it gets here, you will either be happy or unhappy about your career situation. Which would you prefer?

Identify where you would like to be and what you would like to be doing in 10 years. Why should you know where you want to be in 10 years? Because in 10 years you will be somewhere, doing something. Shouldn't it be where and what you want?

The alternative is to buy a lottery ticket and just let things happen.

Lesson 3: Career Focused Questions

The toughest question to answer is the one for which you have no knowledge. Here are some tough questions:

- Where do I want to be in 10 years? How will I get there?

- Where will I end up if I stay in the current career path?

- Am I doing what I really love to do?

- Can I do something else or is it too late?

- Where do I want to be in 10 years?

Only you know what you want in life and in a career. So you need to be honest with yourself and have enough of the right information to make good decisions. Next, you must build a well designed and thought out plan. Then you must carry out that plan until you reach your goal.

If you don't know what you want to be in 10 years, it will require work to figure it out. One way is by taking inventory of your interests and looking at career paths that already exist. It is paramount that you enjoy work and are challenged by it. Otherwise, you won't be superb at it or successful.

Here is a website with tons of useful information about careers: https://www.onetonline.org/.

If you do not know what you want to do, you can take an interest assessment and use the resources on this website: https://www.careeronestop.org/Toolkit/ACINet.aspx.

This website can help you see what other jobs you can do with your current skill set:

https://www.myskillsmyfuture.org/.

Another way of deciding what you want to be in 10 years is by doing short interviews with people at different career levels at work area that interests you–be it Marketing, Engineering, Medicine, Art, whatever. It is easiest to interview people at your current company, but you can talk with anyone you know that works in your career area of interest.

Again, what questions should you ask? Here is a starter list:

- Can you give me an overview of your career and how you got to your current job?

- What do you like about this job?

- What do you dislike?

- If you had to start all over, how would you prepare to have a job like this one?

- What specific skills do you use?

- What skills do you wish you had that you could use?

- If you were in my position, what questions would you ask?

- What else would you like me to know?

- What else? (Continuing to ask "What else" is a subtle way to engage their brainstorming. There may be 10 more "what else" or none. It depends on the person). Always ask this question until the other person runs out of answers.

After the discussion, thank them for their time and expertise. Take good notes and research anything you learned about in the discussion. After two days, send an email thanking them again.

Brainstorming Exercise

Everyone has a little voice that tells them things. You might call this "your subconscious." One of the simplest ways to answer the question of "Where do I want to be in 10 years?" is by brainstorming. Here is one example of brainstorming:

This exercise will help you identify people you know and admire at your company (if employed) or at one of your previous companies. Once you have identified these people, answer this question: What is each of their current job titles? Write the job titles on the worksheet provided. The worksheets are available at coachyourselfbooks.com/worksheets/.

Next, research those identified jobs on the Internet. In the search engine, you can type the job title and the job description and press the Enter key. For example, if one job is a Marketing Director, type "marketing director job description" into the search engine.

The results page should provide many links to current job descriptions in that field of interest. Read several of those descriptions.

Next question: Do 70% of these job descriptions seem like something that would interest you?

If the answer is yes, you can interview people that have that position (see above).

If the answer is no, look at the next job description on your list (worksheet is available online: coachyourselfbooks.com/worksheets/) and repeat the process.

How will I get there?

In Maine, there's a saying: "You can't get there from here." That is also true for plotting your career–you can't plot it from step 1 to step 10 (start to completion). Plot your course in reverse, step 10 to step 1–it is much easier.

For example, to be a Director of Information Technology, you first need to be a Technology Manager. Before you can be a Technology Manager, you need to have some Senior Engineer (either Software, Hardware or Firmware) experience and complete management training (the more formalized the program, the better). To be a Senior Engineer, you first need 5 or more years as an Engineer. To be an Engineer, you first need to have either a strong proven technical background or a Bachelor's of Science in one of the Engineering areas or both. There will be additional skill sets you will need to develop to be fully proficient.

Does that make sense?

If it doesn't make sense, here is one more example: Consider an upside-down pyramid. The top is the largest section titled "Director of Information Technology" and requires the most experience and knowledge. At the bottom is "Engineering Student". You most likely will be in one level between the top and bottom levels. Each job has a description of all required tasks and skills.

Once you identify the tasks and skills, you can put these in your professional development plan, as appropriate, so that when your opportunity arrives, you will have the required skills.

Where will I end up if I stay in the current career path?

An easy way to see a career path is by looking at your business organization and the people more senior than you. You can also look at lateral paths. For example, if you are in Marketing, you could look at a Sales organization and the paths it can provide. If you are an EMT (Emergency Management Technician) but you're tired of riding around in an ambulance all day, you might work in a Hospital Emergency Room and becoming a Nurse.

Where you end up is anyone's guess or a place of your choosing. If you want it to be a place of your choosing, you need an excellent plan. Also, you need a strong network of business and professional contacts (more on that later). This is the best way to get to a place of your choosing.

The destination may change. That's okay. The important thing is to keep moving forward in your chosen direction. If you adapt and react to opportunities and take whatever comes along, you will get somewhere, but it will most likely not be where you want to be. Eventually, you may even box yourself into a corner.

Am I doing what I really love to do?

Your answer should be yes. If it isn't, you need to find something else to do.

If going to work, doesn't "fire up your engines" and get you exciting about the coming day, that's no way to live. But before you leave this job, first determine the cause of your feelings. The reason can be any or all of: the Manager, the Job, or the Company.

It's the Manager

If you're in a position, assess why you are unhappy. If you like the work, but not the person you work for, no worries. Managers don't stay in the same organization long. The average time for a manager is about 18 months.

Likewise, if you love your manager that's fine. Either way, this manager will go somewhere else soon. (See the section on Managing your Manager).

Does that change your perspective on the job you are doing now?

It's the Job

If the problem is the job and not the manager you have several choices. These choices include:

Find another job function that's more interesting in the same organization. Sometimes spending time cross-training in a different job can be an eye-opening, enjoyable and fruitful experience.

You can find another job in another organization at the same company.

You can find another job in another company (but if you like the company, that may not be the best choice).

You can talk with your manager, develop the relationship and trust equity. When the manager leaves, they could take you with them.

Your manager may help you find another job that better suits your interests at the current company.

Does that change your perspective on the job you are doing now?

It's the Company

If the company or its culture is the problem, know this: it will not change and rarely will get better while you are there, unless there has been a large event that's causing a paradigm shift. There are excellent companies, okay companies and companies you should just run from. Sorry, but that's the truth.

What do you do if the company is the problem? That's up to you. If your manager insulates you from most of the problems, consider yourself lucky, those managers are rare. Leaving the company may not be the best choice.

If you're working at a company where management micro-manages everyone, or it's a toxic work environment, the best way to proceed is to update your resume (which should always be up to date), and talk with your friends and outside colleagues about their company. You can do informational interviews with them as discussed previously. Choose your time to leave ONLY after you have found and accepted another job because it is always easier to find a job when you have one.

Often the best jobs found are through other people and they do not advertise these positions to the public. The reason for this is managers like to hire either people they know and trust or by personal referral within their own department.

You can look at company ratings on these sites:

www.GlassDoor.com

www.indeed.com/companies

Either of these sites will tell you the good, the terrible and the downright ugly about almost any company in the United States. Read a lot of the reviews to look for common themes and problems. Don't just look at the number or star ratings. The good stuff you want to know is in the comments that people write.

One thing to keep in mind: no company is perfect, nor are the people that work there. So using sources like Glass Door help narrow down a list of companies to consider. Those websites are not the only source of information. Use your network to find people that work at companies of interest and speak with them about their company. Offer to buy them coffee and meet them as their schedule permits.

Questions (open-ended when possible) to ask:

- Can you give me an idea of what it's like to work at your company?

- How long have you worked there?

- What's the corporate culture like?

- Have you worked with the same people for years, or do people usually move around or leave the company after a year or two there?

- What do you like about this company?

- What do you dislike about this company?

- How long do you think you will work at this company?

- What are the benefits besides salary available at your company? What do you think about those?

Also, ask questions you think are helpful to understand the company. You should know within about 30 minutes if this is a company you want to consider or if it's a company to avoid.

Can I do something else or is it too late?

The short answer is "Yes," you can do something else. Unless you are at the end of your career, it isn't too late (and even then many people create a "second act" or career for themselves). It may take more work, persistence, creativity and lots of thinking, but it's definitely possible to do something else in your career at almost any time.

The important questions to ask yourself are:

- Why am I asking this question?

- Why am I unhappy or unfulfilled?

- Am I prepared to do the work it will take to change careers?

- What do I know about the career of interest?

Summary

In your career, it is very important to have a 10-year plan. Build the plan in reverse so you start with the end goal and work your way back to your current position. Define requirements and skills you must gain for each step of the plan.

Only you will make your success happen. The way you make it happen is by asking the right questions and acting on the answers you learn.

If you are unhappy at work, it is important for you to figure out why–It isn't always the company.

You can change your career and life. It is up to you.

Questions to Ask Yourself

- Do I have a 10-year plan?

- Am I keeping this plan updated?

- If I could develop one skill this year, what would that be?

- If I could change one thing in my career this year, what would that be?

- Are there any obstacles to my adding a skill or changing one thing? If so, how can I overcome those obstacles?

Additional Resources

- Forbes Magazine-"Changing Careers: Signs You're Ready For A Change, And How To Make It Happen"

- Glassdoor.com-"6 Things You *Don't* Want to Hear About Changing Careers (But Need to Anyway)"

- TheBalanceCareers.com – "10 Steps to a Successful Career Change"

Chapter 4: The Right Decisions

"Sometimes it's the smallest decisions that can change your life forever."

~ Keri Russell

Lesson 4: Improve Your Methods for Decision Making

Few things in life affect you more than the decisions you make. Any decision can change the course of your life. You need to learn how to make the best logical decisions with all the information. The result of your decisions should be the result you desire.

The larger and more important the decision, the more time and effort you should put into the decision-making process.

Here are the steps (and an example) for making excellent decisions:

1. Identify the decision you want to make and your ideal outcomes and objectives.

   - John wants to buy a car for only $10,000.
   - John needs to decide what car to buy and whether to finance it or pay cash.
   - John has $10,000 in savings and good credit.

2. Research. Put together as much information about the subject as you can, to improve your chances of making an informed decision.

   - John researches all used and new cars to fully understand the strengths and weaknesses.
   - John researches interest rates for new and used vehicles.

3. Define all choices. Keep all choices that align with your interests, values, and goals. Discard the rest.

   - What's important to John is the car's reliability, safety, and fuel efficiency, not the make or model.
   - What's important to John regarding cost is that he

doesn't want to pay a loan for over 2 years.

4. Define all outcomes of each option.

- John could buy a new car, but that would cost $20,000 or more and he would have to pay for it for 5 years.
- John could buy a used car and pay cash, but then he would have nothing remaining in savings.
- John could buy a used car, pay for part of it and finance the rest. That way he could keep enough money in savings.

5. Define all the pros and cons of each outcome.

- John would love a beautiful new car, but can't afford to buy it; it's just too expensive.
- He could buy a used car if it is in good shape; he might have to worry about more repairs.
- Ideally, John would like the car to look almost new.
- John can't pay all cash, because he needs reserve savings in case of an emergency.

6. Ask trusted family and friends for their opinion on the choices.

- His brother says "go for the new car, you deserve it!"
- His father says, "buy a used car, just make sure it's a one-owner car, with only 50,000 miles, and no history of accidents or flood damage."
- His girlfriend doesn't care what he buys; she wants the radio to have Bluetooth, so she can play her music.

7. Make your decision.

- John buys a one-owner, Toyota Camry, with 50,000 miles, a clean title that's free of accidents and weather damage.
- He puts $5,000 down on the car and finances the rest of the balance for 2 years at 5% interest.
- He buys new floor mats to make it look like a new car.
- The radio has no Bluetooth, but no one gets everything they want.

In the example above, John could have made a different decision. The decision he made was one that met all his requirements and was the best overall choice for a car. Long term he will know if he made the best decision.

This is one process for making excellent decisions. Sometimes, even with this process, you can have an unexpected result. However, this process should limit risk and maximize the chance of a good result.

Decision Trees and Flow Charts

Decision trees and flowcharts are very helpful for making good decisions. These are excellent because both will visually engage your thought process.

They often use decision trees and flowcharts in technical disciplines to find the best solution. But there's no reason you can't use these tools when making an important decision.

According to Wikipedia, "A decision tree is a decision support tool that uses a tree-like model of decisions and their consequences, including chance event outcomes, resource costs, and utility."

According to SmartDraw.com, a "flowchart is a visual representation of the sequence of steps and decisions needed to perform a process. It notes each step in the sequence within a diagram shape. Steps are linked by connecting lines and directional arrows."

Since there are so many excellent resources online, this book won't cover much more about these tools. The important concept is the more information you have and the better you identify outcomes (best and worst outcomes), the better decisions you will make for difficult and complex issues.

You can create decision trees and flowcharts with a pencil and paper or on a whiteboard with dry markers. You don't have to buy any software to do this (although a lot of this software is fun to use and can make the process easier). Below are great resources with a lot more information.

Summary

- Few things will affect your life more than your decisions.

- The larger and more important the decision, the more time and effort you should put into the decision-making process.

- It is paramount that you develop a reliable method for making excellent decisions.

Questions to Ask Yourself

- Do I make good decisions? If not, why not?
- What can I do now to make better decisions?
- Do I always want to learn from my own mistakes?
- What is the last thing I learned the hard way?
- What other decisions could I have made?

- Would the outcome have been any different?

Additional Resources

- Psychology Today – "5 Tips for Better Decision Making"

Using Decision Trees

- Wikipedia – https://en.wikipedia.org/wiki/Decision_tree

- LucidChart.com – https://www.lucidchart.com/pages/decision-tree?a=1

- Victor Lavrenko YouTube, Decision trees – https://www.youtube.com/watch?v=eKD5gxPPeY0

Using Flowcharts

- SmartDraw.com – https://www.smartdraw.com/flowchart/

- Wikipedia – https://en.wikipedia.org/wiki/Flowchart

- Eugene O'Loughlin Video re Flowcharts – https://www.youtube.com/watch?v=hN9xemJYwos

Chapter 5: Perform a SWOT Analysis

Good leaders make people's strengths effective and their weaknesses irrelevant.

~ Frances Hesselbein

Lesson 5: Understand Your Strengths and Opportunities

Taking inventory of your abilities and liabilities is very important. You should understand your gifts: the strengths and opportunities that make you who you are and what is unique about you! Using a SWOT analysis is one way to accomplish that task.

What the Heck is a SWOT?

They use a SWOT analysis or matrix for business strategic planning. It identifies the strengths, weaknesses, opportunities, and threats related to achieving a specific project, business initiative or analyzing market competition. A SWOT analysis is also useful to identify the same four categories as those apply to you and your career.

The best way to do a SWOT analysis is with someone you trust that knows you well. It is very difficult to see oneself the way others can. However, you can do an initial evaluation (write it down) to a "straw dog" to start a discussion.

Evaluate Your Strengths

Strengths are what you do well. Said another way, these are your talents and abilities. We gravitate towards our strengths in both our personal lives (such as hobbies) and professional lives (in choosing a career). Think about it: Shouldn't we gravitate towards our best assets? Who would want to focus on their own weaknesses?

For example, if you are good at math, you might find music and games like chess interesting. If you are good at Math, you might also do well in Engineering, Logistics, Economics or Business or Web Analytics.

Evaluate Your Weaknesses

Weaknesses are the lack of abilities, skills or traits that could put you at a disadvantage, when compared to others. For example, if you want to be a Digital Director, but know little about technology, Search Engine Optimization (SEO) or Email Campaigns, these are weaknesses. When identified, you can turn some of your weaknesses into strengths by taking training and working on projects that use those skills.

Sometimes, however, weaknesses are just that–weaknesses. For example, if you are bad with numbers, you would probably be very unhappy working in a Finance or Accounting department.

When to do Something About Your Weaknesses

The only time you need to work on weaknesses is if those are keeping you from being successful in your long-term goals. Otherwise, don't focus on them. We are all weak at something.

Evaluate Your Opportunities

Opportunities are the things you can do that will aid you in building the career you want. For example, you might have a lack of experience in public speaking or presenting to large crowds. To help build your public speaking skills, you could join Toastmasters. You would gain public speaking skills and develop an entirely new network of professional colleagues.

Here's another example: You're interested in working at a company that uses only Apple computers, but you only know how to use Windows computers. The opportunity is to learn how to use Apple computers before you interview or work there.

Evaluate Your Threats

Threats can be people at work, the state of the industry you work in, the unemployment rate, or anything else that can harm your career. By identifying these threats, you can plan out a strategy to minimize potential liabilities.

For example, if you want to build new automobiles, but those jobs are going overseas or done by robots, you will probably have to seek a luxury or custom brand manufacturer and spend several years as an apprentice or go to a specialized technical school before you can do that.

The important thing about threats is to identify those as soon as you can to minimize risk and continue along your 10-year career plan.

Put it All Together

Your SWOT analysis is done and you have all kinds of good information. How do you use all this SWOT information?

First, look at the below SWOT analysis table:

	HELPFUL	**HARMFUL**
Internal (to you)	Strengths (good)	Weaknesses (bad)
External (to you)	Opportunities (good)	Threats (bad)

Notice the areas that are "helpful" and "harmful." In life, always focus mostly on your strengths and opportunities. Not only will you be happier-you will be more successful.

Strengths and Opportunities

Strengths and Opportunities are the areas you want to build a career around. It is important to know what your strengths are because these should align well with whatever career you choose. Again, build on your strengths and interests. This will enable you to have a wonderful, fulfilling career.

Weaknesses and Threats

Weaknesses and Threats cause people problems in life and in the workplace. It is important to identify these so you can avoid or fix those things. In your career, consider how to eliminate or minimize weaknesses or threats, so you can be more successful. Again, should you only mitigate a weakness or threat if these will cause problems in your 10-year plan. Otherwise, don't worry about them.

For example, if one of your weaknesses is listening to people, you definitely want to fix that. This weakness could definitely harm your career if unresolved. Take a class or read a book on actively listening.

If one of your weaknesses is creating custom graphics and your job is Technical Writer with a career goal of being a Technical Documentation Director, you probably don't have to worry too much about that weakness. Graphics departments usually help create those images.

Job Searches

Taking a good SWOT inventory is also important for job searching. Your strengths are key assets. Your resume should highlight these, so employers will easily understand your competencies.

Summary

- Taking inventory of your abilities and liabilities is very important. Using a SWOT analysis is one way to accomplish that task.

- Build your life and career around your strengths and opportunities.

- Minimize the liability of your weaknesses and threats.

Questions to Ask Yourself

Regarding Strengths

- What are the most important strengths relevant to my particular career path?

- Which strengths do I need to develop in the next year?

Regarding Weaknesses

- What weaknesses are important for my career path?

- Which ones must I fix in the next year?

- Who could be a resource for minimizing these weaknesses?

Regarding Opportunities

- Which opportunities are important to my 10-year plan?

- Which ones should I work on the next year?

Regarding Threats

Which threats could harm my career plans?

Which ones should I mitigate in the next year?

- Who could be a resource for minimizing these threats?

Additional Resources

- Wikipedia.org-"SWOT Analysis"

- Mindtools.com-"Personal SWOT Analysis: Making the Most of Your Talents and Opportunities"

- Strengths Finder 2.0–This book and the accompanying test will objectively help you understand your strengths so you can make the most of those.

Chapter 6: Sincere Feedback

"Critique, feedback, reaction to one's work or the way they have presented it, regardless of intention, is a gift."

~ Mark Brand

Lesson 6: Ask Colleagues for Sincere Feedback

This task will require you to "check your ego at the door." Asking someone else what they think of you takes a LOT of nerve–because the answers you'll get will not be the ones you expect. It is, however, the best source of truth for how others see and perceive your abilities and behaviors.

This is how to solicit personal feedback: Select 10 people you know from work and trust; email each of them. In the email, you can say something like the following (The worksheets are available at coachyourselfbooks.com/worksheets/):

In the Subject line type: I'd like to get your opinion on something

Hi <the person's name>,

Thanks for reading this email. I was wondering if you would do me a favor. I am trying to get honest feedback on the top 2 or 3 areas of improvement I could focus on in the coming year. I am sending you this because I know and trust you. Hopefully, if your answer is yes, you'll think about it and send me some helpful feedback. You can also mention things I do well, but that's not the point of my email.

Anything you say will be truly appreciated and it won't hurt my feelings. Please be "brutally honest" with me.

Thank you in advance,

<your name>

Response rates to this email will vary. If you know these people well, you can expect about a 20 to 30 percent answer rate. If you don't work with these people, the rate may be even higher. Either way, it's an excellent source of information.

It is very difficult to read and accept constructive criticism about oneself. However, it is the only way to learn how others see you. It takes a high level of maturity to hear these things. But I guarantee you it will be worth it.

When you get a response, thank the sender. Allow your mind a day or two to evaluate the feedback. If you get a few responses that echo similar themes, consider working on those issues. You can ask for additional information from the sender, but if you have lots of questions or complex ones, you might invite that person to lunch (your treat), to get more insight and network.

Summary

- It takes a lot of maturity and self-confidence to ask others for feedback about areas of improvement.

- You will learn more about yourself from others than you will ever by thinking about yourself.

Questions to Ask Yourself

- Am I prepared to hear negative feedback about myself?

- What do I think are the top 2 or 3 areas I could focus on in the next year?

- Who are 10 people I believe I can get honest feedback from?

- Am I ready to work on areas of myself? If not, why not?

Additional Resources

- Harvard Business Review – "How to Handle Negative Feedback"

- Forbes Magazine – "8 Ways Negative Feedback Can Lead to Greater Success at Work"

- Fast Company – "Thick Skin Thinking: How to Use Negative Feedback at Work to Your Advantage"

Chapter 7: No Substitute For Excellent Planning

"Planning is bringing the future into the present so that you can do something about it now."

~ Alan Lakein

Lesson 7: You Must Plan Out Your Career Now!

All successes begin with a great plan; that's the purpose of this chapter. Planning isn't difficult, it's only a series of steps (actions) and milestones (accomplishments).

Once you have answered all the tough questions and done a good SWOT analysis to create a well thought out career plan. The plan should comprise a 10-year plan, broken down into 1-year chunks. The best way to accomplish something important is with a plan that's written and reviewed consistently.

With a plan, you can measure progress to assure you are moving towards your goal. Without a plan, you will have no way to measure this journey, nor an easy way to tell if you are on track or going in the wrong direction.

This plan is for your use only. You can share it with others, but that's not the purpose. You will control, measure and update it as necessary to achieve all that you desire.

Some companies have formal career planning and employee reviews. This is separate from the planning discussed here, because you need to track your career progress over many years, regardless of the employer.

Quarterly, Annual Reviews and Updates

Once you develop and put in place a career plan, schedule time throughout the year to update and measure your progress. Appointments are 1 hour for a quarterly review and 2 hours for the annual review.

Set up appointments in your personal calendar (like a Google Calendar) not your work calendar (like your company's Outlook). Make these appointments automatically. That way you create only 4 appointments: March 15 (quarterly review), June

15 (quarterly review), September 15 (quarterly review) and December 15 (annual review), that repeat for the next 10 years.

Quarterly Review

At the quarterly review, look at your plan and determine if you have completed the correct percentage of each of the planned tasks. For example, if it is March 15, and you have scheduled one year for a specific training, you should be 25 percent complete with that training.

It's okay if you don't have every task completed up to the scheduled amount. The important thing here is to raise your awareness of what progress you have made towards this year's plan and what's left to accomplish for the year. This review can also get you back on track if you've off track.

After you have gone through the list of actions for the quarter, the review is done until the next quarter.

Annual Review

The annual or end of the year review is an opportunity to look over the progress you have made in the past year. Planning and execution is hard work. Celebrate all your past year's successes.

Identify tasks not completed and discern the worth of these tasks. If these tasks are still worthwhile, schedule those in next year's plan. If these tasks are now not worthwhile or relevant, make a note stating what you accomplished towards this task and why you have discontinued it.

Each year you can review not only the current year's accomplishments, but the prior year's. By reviewing your progress, you will see trends. Compare one year to another and to gain insights about other things you need to learn to increase your skill set.

Look at what needs to be accomplished in the following year towards completion of the 10-year plan (again another 1-year chunk of the plan).

After you have charted out next year's plan, put it aside for a day or two to give yourself time to think about it. Updated it when you are ready. Then work that plan!

Lesson 8: Understand Professional Career Tracks

There are two types of roles in any company or organization: Individual Contributor and Management.

Individual Contributor (IC)

The Individual Contributor (IC) is a specialist that focuses on one job. People in these roles work by themselves or as part of a team, to create some kind of work product. That person does not have to manage or supervise employees, nor manage budgets.

Management

Any time you add the word Manager to a job title it means that a person may have to manage people, processes, budgets and/or other things in the work environment. Management isn't for everyone. A Manager usually comes from an Individual Contributor role where she has already been a specialist in an area that's managed by this role. For example, before she became an Information Technology (IT) Manager, first she was a software developer; before she became an Account Manager, she was a Sales Support Specialist.

Promotions and Raises

More and more companies today create pools of Individual Contributors and assign those to a project rather than one department with one Manager. If you decide you don't want to manage people, you can stay an Individual Contributor and progress in your career (with promotions and raises) without having to go into management to get a promotion. Going into management to get promoted is a terrible idea, especially, if you have no management training and are not interested in helping people.

The management question you should ask is: Do I like people enough to spend 70% of my time working on people, relationships and communication issues, and enforcing policies from upper management? If the answer is yes, you might be a good candidate for management. If the answer is no, remain an Individual Contributor.

Summary

- All successes usually begin with a great plan.

- Quarterly reviews are an opportunity to see if you're on track for the year and to make corrections as necessary.

- Annual reviews are an opportunity to celebrate your successes, highlight the objectives you missed and to map out next year's plan.

- There are two types of roles at companies: Individual Contributors and Management. Each type of role has its rewards and challenges.

Questions to Ask Yourself

- Have I ever tried planning out my career in the past? If so, and it didn't work, why did it not work? What will I do differently this time?

- What are my worries about career planning?

- How will I keep myself accountable on a quarterly and annual basis?

- Do I have any other concerns about doing this? If so, what can I do now to resolve those concerns?

- Do I think I will get any career planning support from my management?

Additional Resources

- Linkedin.com – "IC or People Manager...?"

- Harvard Business Review – "Do You Have a Manager's Mindset"

- New York Times – "Maybe Management Isn't Your Style"

Chapter 8: Basic Survival Skills for Business

"Opportunities are usually disguised as hard work, so most people don't recognize them."

~ Ann Landers

There are skills and attributes each person should have to survive and thrive in today's work world, regardless of the company size. These skills can improve with time and practice.

Lesson 9: Be Willing to Pay the Price

In your life and career, there will always be a price to pay. If you pay the price now, it's done. If you don't pay now, you may pay it for the rest of your life. No one is exempt from paying their dues—it's just the way the world works.

Here is a financial example: When you purchase a home you can get a 15-year or 30-year mortgage. The longer you pay, the more it will cost you in interest. It will cost you approximately twice as much for a 30-year mortgage as it would for a 15 year one. It is this way because of the factor of time—the longer you borrow money from the bank, the more you'll pay for it.

It is the same way for life and career: You can pay the price now for something, or later. Paying later will always cost you more.

What is this price I'm talking about?

"The price" is the work you do and the sacrifices you make to achieve your 10-year career plan. If you want to be a Marketing Director in 10 years and already have a job in marketing, the price you pay might be getting an MBA in Marketing. If you have the college education, but not the job, it could mean taking a lower level job in a marketing or sales department to learn everything about a company's products and services and gaining additional skills on your path to becoming a Marketing Director.

Paying the Price now increases the likelihood you will achieve your goals and achieve those sooner.

Lesson 10: Preparation

Always prepare well. This may seem like an easy choice, but in today's world, lots of people don't understand or embrace this concept.

- Are you always prepared with your work? If not, why?

- Do you always meet assigned deadlines? If not, why?

Being a professional means always being prepared. If you have an assignment or your manager or client has an expectation, you will complete something on a certain date, you need to meet that expectation.

Winging It

Many people don't fully prepare their work. They make excuses for not meeting their deadlines, or ignore those deadlines altogether and assume that they aren't accountable. The worst scenarios for this is when they "wing it" and get caught.

A manager may say "it's okay, you can get it to me tomorrow," to someone who misses a deadline, but what she is thinking is that "you screwed up and now I have to wait, which won't help you when you need something." You should embrace this concept. Managers hate surprises (more on that later in the book).

Lesson 11: No Excuses

No excuses are acceptable. Not in the real world. Said another way: there's no excuse for an excuse-managers and others really don't want to hear it.

If you often make excuses, this is an opportunity for you to change your work habits.

What you need to ask yourself is:

- Why can't I meet my deadlines?

- Why don't I follow through with my responsibilities?

- What could help me perform better?

- Should I seek guidance from a peer or manager?

If the reason for missing a deadline is the amount of work, a lack of knowledge or skill set or the work environment, you must talk with your manager about it. That's why she is there—to remove roadblocks and to help you become successful.

With all of that said, you may already know you need to do this and not care. If you don't love or at least like what you are doing, go do something else. Your life and happiness are too important to waste. Not meeting goals and deadlines will only make you and your management miserable.

The questions you could ask yourself are:

- What would make me want to change and meet these responsibilities and deadlines?

- Where better could I apply my skills?

- What other types of jobs would make me happier?

All jobs aren't right for all people. If you are in this situation, you have the power to change it.

Lesson 12: Build Trust

Trust is very difficult to earn in today's world because many people lie all the time! It really is unbelievable. Maybe the reason is that it's easier and they don't think they will get caught. The lack of honesty is so pervasive, always inspect closely to be sure you know the truth.

People who always prepare gain one of the most valuable rewards from their manager and coworkers: high trust equity. This is priceless. Trust isn't something you can buy, you must earn it. Once earned, it can be a bridge to wonderful things in your career, that you never imagined! However, if you lose trust, it is very difficult to regain.

Where did This Start?

Where did the lack of being prepared and missing deadlines start? Maybe it began in childhood when everyone would get a trophy and called a winner, regardless of the effort they put into the competition, regardless of their skill. It is the false narrative that "Everyone is a Winner."

In real life, "Everyone is NOT a Winner." There are winners and losers, which is the way it has always been. If you want to progress, if you want to be an all-star, if you want to be a "Winner," you must produce, meet your deadlines and build trust with your management and peers.

Summary

- To be successful in life, you need to meet your commitments and other's expectations.

- The price you pay now will always be less than the price you pay later.

- No one cares about excuses for not meeting your obligations.

- Nothing is more important in relationships than building trust.

- Not everyone in the real world is a winner.

Questions to Ask Yourself

- Am I willing to pay the price to be successful? Do I think I can do it? How will I keep myself motivated throughout the year?

- Am I always prepared for work and my other obligations?

- Am I willing to do whatever it takes to get the job done, or do I slide through life and work?

- How often do I justify why I didn't make a deadline or an obligation?

- Do people trust me? At work? In my life?

- Am I a winner?

- If I am not a winner yet, what would it take to become one?

Additional Resources

- InspireForLifeCoaching.com – "4 Powerful Benefits of Being Prepared"

- Medium.com – "If You Want Success, Figure Out the Price, Then Pay It"

- Forbes Magazine – "The 8 Most Damaging Excuses People Make For Their Unhappiness"

- Psychology Today – 5 Ways to Build Trust and Honesty in Your Relationships"

- Forbes Magazine – "Growing Up Where Everyone is a Winner–How do Kids Learn to Win?"

Lesson 13: Become a Specialist

As stated previously, Individual Contributors and Management are the two professional tracks most often seen in business. It used to be that these roles were mutually exclusive, meaning that managers just managed, they didn't do the work, because they spent the majority of their time planning and in meetings. That is no longer the case as more and more companies are looking for "hands-on managers" that can do both, when needed.

Another fact that's well known to Managers, but not necessarily to Individual Contributors, is that Managers usually come from the Specialist ranks (especially in technology, finance, accounting, marketing, and human resources). This is because specialists are experts in an area. There's a school of thought that firmly believes only an expert can manage an expert. So it's recommended that you: Become a Specialist and keep competency in that area as long as you are in business.

One of the great things about being a specialist is that you can pursue an Individual Contributor career path and if you decide you want to try Management, you can do that too with some training. Then if you later decide you don't want to be a manager, you can go back to being a Specialist. The same is not true for the Generalist.

Generalists can be highly effective managers, but as Individual Contributors they often run into a hiring manager's perception of "we don't understand what you do and we need a specific skill set, so we will hire the Specialist." The only exception to this is working in small business. In a small business, a Generalist is valuable because his wide array of skills is needed, expected and a true asset to the company.

More and more of today's companies are paying specialists for work when they need them. Specialists are in high demand because employers can quantify their skill sets to current tasks and projects.

Summary

- Become a specialist in one or two things to increase your chances of being employed.

- Generalists are much harder for employers to quantify for Individual Contributor (IC) roles.

- Specialists can become management with the right training.

Questions to Ask Yourself

- Am I a specialist? If so, do I have any interest in learning about other areas I could work in?

- Am I a generalist? If so, has being a generalist hurt me in my career path?

- If I am not a specialist, do I want to become one? If yes, in what field and what training/education is required to achieve that?

Additional Resources

- Fast Company – "What You Should Know About Being a Specialist or Generalist"

- Monster.com – "Should I Become a Specialist or Generalist?"

- Cleverism.com – "The Ultimate Career Choice– Generalist or Specialist"

Lesson 14: Under Promise, Over Deliver

Setting realistic timelines is paramount, not only for good planning, but to set the correct expectation of your client, stakeholder or manager. One way to do this is to under promise, over deliver.

The saying "under promise, over deliver" comes from the Technology sector. The purpose of it isn't to slack off. The purpose of it is to set realistic deadlines for commitments that are achievable. Business usually wants a technology solution in their time frame (which is typically faster than technology can build it). Technology projects usually take longer than expected, because of the unexpected things that happen with software, people and the shifting demands of the business.

A person who over-commits for a deliverable is seen as someone that can't meet deadlines or commitments. No matter how good their intentions, they should have planned better and added time for the unexpected (often called Murphy's Law).

Setting realistic timelines or commitments is about doing an accurate, well thought out plan and estimate. Adding 10% for the unexpected and delivering on that commitment is acceptable and people will appreciate it. If you do this planning consistently over time, you will build substantial trust equity.

There is an old saying in business "If you want something done, give it to the busiest person." That isn't accurate anymore. It's up to the individual to push back and set realistic expectations for management, clients, and stakeholders, because what they really want is consistency, quality and predictability.

Summary

- It's up to you to negotiate realistic deadlines with your manager and others.

- Avoid the urge to over-promise or commit–especially if you already have a full workload.

- Plan at 100%, then add 10% for the unexpected.

- Deadlines and expectations need to be reasonable and achievable, not early or unrealistic

- No one wants to miss a deadline. It takes maturity to negotiable a realistic, achievable deadline that will provide the finished work product and the right level of quality desired.

Questions to Ask Yourself

- Do I have problems negotiating and meeting deadlines?

- Do I commit to too many things and then not get all completed on time?

- Do I plan for the unexpected?

- Has not completing projects on time hurt my career?

- What can I do to change my situation?

Additional Resources

- WikiQuotes.org – "Murphy's Law"

- Tom Peters – "Under Promise, Over Deliver"

- IvyExec.com – "7 Things to Say to a Boss With Unrealistic Expectations"

- EatYourCareer.com – "How to Manage and Renegotiate Deadlines in the Workplace"

Lesson 15: One Hour A Day: Continuous Learning

Technology and knowledge change quickly. To stay current with information and progress in your area of work, dedicate one hour a day for study per day. There really is no other way to stay current and to learn new skills.

Ideally, your management will support your study of one hour a day to keep up with technology and knowledge. Those employers that don't support continuous learning will probably lose employees to better and smarter companies and managers.

Another opportunity for learning is cross-training. The benefit of this is learning another person's job in your department. This creates a multiple of opportunities: it enables you to learn new skills and it provides the employer with a backup person, in case the primary person is out of the office. It is a real win-win that's very actionable.

Another opportunity for learning is free online college courses that can provide you with actionable knowledge in a specific area. Also available are learning web sites that have literally thousands of courses with excellent materials for a very low cost.

If your company has a modern work environment, it may also have its own "online university" where you can take courses. Have a discussion with your manager and get his thoughts on the one hour a day learning. He may even have better ideas for you.

If management won't support you in this effort, rather than taking a lunch, consider studying through lunch while you eat. There are plenty of companies out there that support these types of learning initiatives.

Lesson 16: Read-Think-Do

The "Read-Think-Do" method is a fantastic way to learn. You use this in the following way:

Read about a subject, for example, how to stream digital entertainment.

Think about what you have read and maybe look at it again, and

Do the task – in this case, sign up to stream digital entertainment and start binge-watching your favorite shows.

This is the fastest way to learn new things, successfully apply those skills and place that knowledge into long-term memory.

Read-Think-Do is the easiest and quickest way to gain "actionable knowledge." It's probably 1000 times faster than any college course you'll ever take.

Summary

- Studying one hour a day to keep up with technology and knowledge is paramount. Use the Read-Think-Do method for long-term memory retention of newly learned concepts.

- If you don't spend one hour a day learning, your knowledge might become out of date.

- Good companies see this as an excellent idea because they know people are their number one strength and asset.

Questions to Ask Yourself

- Do I study for one hour a day to keep up with technology and knowledge?

- Have I talked to my manager about this?

- What is my company's policy about "continuous learning?"

Additional Resources

- Linkedin.com – "7 Reasons That Continuous Learning is Important"

- TD.org – "10 ways to Build a Culture of Continuous Learning"

- Harvard Business Review – "Automation Will Make Lifelong Learning a Necessary Part of Work"

Lesson 17: Money

Your job must always be about the money, it can't be about anything else.

Many years ago at a corporate meeting of Nortel Networks, a Division Vice President was speaking about the division's annual results. One thing he said was memorable: "Never forget that you work for your family, you don't work for this company – we pay you for part of your life."

Take this to heart: You work for your family and yourself. The company only pays for part of your life. Never forget that.

That's why it always has to be about the money for a job. Companies need to pay you fairly all the time because you only have a limited amount of time to earn money.

For example, if they hire you as a software programmer and the pay is $80,000, that works out to $40 an hour which is low for a talented developer. If however, your company expects you to work 60 hours a week, you are now being paid at a rate of $26.66 an hour. Is that fair? No. There has to be a balance; there has to be equity for you.

Consider this: You can't put a price on life; you can't put a price on a family, but work? You definitely can put a price on that and you should, or you are being foolish. If my saying that makes you angry, good. If you have any doubts about why you are working, just ask your spouse, mate or parents. Trust me, they will tell you. Quickly.

Yes, there should be things about your career that are very important:

- You need to enjoy your work

- You need to like the people you work with

- Your work needs to be challenging so you can grow your professional skills and intellect

- Your company needs to have growth potential for you to progress

- Your company needs to be financially stable

But first, you need to be paid fairly for your work.

Summary

- You need to be paid well and correctly for your work. You are worth it. If you don't do something about any pay inequity you experience, no one else will do it for you.

- You work for your family, not the company. They pay for part of your life. And the last time they checked, no company can give you that time back, if you are not paid appropriately.

Questions to Ask Yourself

- Do I believe that I should be paid that well for my work? Or, do I think I am not worth it?

- If I think I am not worth it why? What can I do to change that perception?

- Who do I work for?

- Who should I work for?

Additional Resources

To find out competitive salaries for your profession, check out www.Salary.com.

For more information about negotiating salaries and raises, check out these articles:

- Glassdoor.com – "How to Negotiate Beyond the Raise You Were Offered"

- Themuse.com – "How to Negotiate Salary: 37 Tips You Need to Know"

Lesson 18: Politics and Religion

Divisive subjects are very difficult and dangerous in the workplace. Here's a little insight: No one knows what you are thinking until you say something or make an expression on your face. Knowing this should insulate you from worrying about topics that are controversial.

It seems like in today's world almost every social topic or controversy is acceptable and defended. That makes it very difficult to express one's opinion if you disagree with someone. In the workplace or with people you work with, the best way is to avoid talking about all these issues, whether it's Politics, Religion, Race, Gender Identification or anything else that's a hot button topic. Doing this won't make you weak; it will make you smart and easier to work with.

The workplace is for work. If you want to have a discussion about anything other than work, do that in your private life and not in the workplace. What you need to understand is that no one in the workplace wants to hear what you have to say about social issues, especially if you disagree with them.

If someone tries to talk with you about social issues of any kind, either just don't respond (that's usually best) or if they push you for a response just say "thanks, but I don't talk about those issues at work." Then change the subject. If you can say that statement with a considerate or kind tone in your voice and no expression on your face that's even better.

The people that do best in corporate and company climates are the ones that are savvy enough to leave their opinions on things not work-related, outside of work.

The workplace is for work, not discussions about politics and religion.

Lesson 19: Dating People You Work With (Co-Workers)

It used to be that companies never allowed employees to date other employees (coworkers) from the workplace. Now with company policies changing more and more, some are allowing this practice, provided that there's no manager-employee relationship of the two people involved.

My thought on dating someone you work with: Don't do it! Never! Not under any circumstances! (If it looks like I am shouting here, it is because I am).

There's a reason people say it's a bad idea; it is because it is a bad idea.

Consider this: If you date someone that lives in the apartment next to your apartment, where do you go, if the relationship doesn't work out? You can't go home, that's where the other person lives!

Like any other decision you make in life or business, first, consider the consequences before you do something. If dating someone you work with doesn't work out, what's the worst that can happen? Not only can it totally blow up your work relationship and make it a difficult place to work for you, but it can also bring unnecessary drama into an otherwise amiable workplace.

So, it's not a matter of you can't date a co-worker; it's that you should not date them.

Summary

- Dating a co-worker is always a bad idea.

- Don't mix your professional life with your personal life.

Questions to Ask Yourself

- Have I ever dated someone at work? If so, how did it end?

- Would I ever consider dating a co-worker? If so, why?

- Am I currently in a relationship with a co-worker? What worries do I have about it affecting my job?

- Is anyone else at work dating a co-worker? If so, and that has ended, how did it end? What vibe or feeling is in the office now because of that personal relationship?

Additional Resources

- Monster.com – Danger: Office Romance Ahead

- Readers Digest – 10 Things You Must Think of Before Dating a Co-worker

- US News & World Report – "Office Romance 101: What if You Are Dating the Boss?"

- Monster.ca – "When Your Boss Dates a Co-Worker"

Lesson 20: The Caffeine Effect

Caffeine is a drug; a powerful drug. Most people underestimate caffeine's power and effect on human behavior. It's so powerful on the mind and body, it is surprising that more people are not aware of all its negative effects.

That said, if you are a person who's frequently anxious, hyper, agitated or finds it difficult to concentrate at work, consider reducing your caffeine intake (If you drink coffee, tea or sodas). If you have any of the symptoms mentioned above, also talk with your doctor about it.

Employers often put coffee makers, tea and soda machines in the break room as a benefit for employees. Employers do that with the best of intentions, but it's up to you to figure out if caffeine does or doesn't work well for your body and mind. If it doesn't work well for you, consider avoiding it.

Summary

- Caffeine is a very strong drug. Not everyone functions well with too much of it.

- If you have any of caffeine's symptoms mentioned above, also talk with your doctor about it.

Questions to Ask Yourself

- Do I drink over 2 cups of regular coffee, tea or caffeinated soda a day?

- Do I find my hands shaking sometimes for no reason during the workday?

- Do I get edgy, tense or anxious for no reason during the workday?

- Do I find myself sweating or heart racing for no reason during the workday?

- Do I have difficulty concentrating during the workday?

Additional Resources

- Healthline – "The Effects of Caffeine on Your Body"

- Mayo Clinic – "Caffeine: How much is too much?"

- WebMD-"Caffeine"

Lesson 21: Most Powerful Person in Room

Whether you are new to an organization or not, it is very important that you understand and can identify who is the most powerful person in the room. It isn't always the person who's speaking, and it's not necessarily the person leading the meeting.

The best way to know is to ask your colleagues when you have a moment alone with them. There's a hierarchy in most companies and the sooner you learn the hierarchy and who the real power people are, the better prepared you will be to avoid making a mistake or saying the wrong thing.

In meetings, the easiest way to tell who wields that real power is by looking at everyone's body language, who they are pointed towards and who they are looking at, regardless of who is speaking. Typically, people focus their attention on the most powerful person.

The most powerful person usually isn't the person who does most of the talking. It is usually the person who does most listening in meetings. Also, it's not true that the most powerful person is the one that has the highest level job title.

You can learn more about an organization and its people by listening in meetings and saying little. As the saying goes "If you are speaking, you can't be listening."

Summary

- It is always very important to know who is the real power in the room.

- Understanding your organization's hierarchy is critical.

Questions to Ask Yourself

- Have I ever searched for the power in the room?

- How often have I been right about who has the power?

- Have I ever talked with someone about the hierarchy and people in my company?

Additional Resources

- Linkedin.com-"Understanding Human Dynamics~ An Essential Skill for the New Workplace"

- Forbes.com-"What I Learned About Office Politics That Changed My Career"

Lesson 22: Know How vs. Know Who

There are many people who say it's not what you know, it's who you know. If you had to guess which is more important, "what you know or who you know", what would you say?

If you said "who you know," yes, you are correct. But "what you know" is also important. You need to know both to be really successful in your career. Long term, one without the other isn't enough.

If you know a lot about your job and are busily working away without coming out of your cube to talk with people, you will never progress in your career. Likewise, if you are working late to impress your boss and the boss has gone home, how will he know? He won't.

Steven Covey in his 1990s book, "7 Habits of Highly Effective People" talks about "making regular deposits in the emotional bank account." Unless you spend time with people, get to know them and build a relationship, you'll have no one who will help you when you need help. Any library you go to will most likely have a copy of this book.

For those people who like a great story and networking information, read this book: "The Celestine Prophecy." This is an enjoyable networking book and a quick read.

If you're always networking but incompetent at your job, you will also fail long term. Short term you may make inroads, but today's workplace requires hands on people at all levels. Networking is very important, but that alone won't be enough to build an excellent career. You must also have a solid foundation of skills and work.

The importance of quality work in business is so important that companies have been bringing jobs back to the United States because the quality of work in China and India is so poor and the rate of defects are so high. One case for this is Generac, a company that had gone to China and closed plants in the US. They found it was actually more cost effective to produce their products in Wisconsin because of the high percentage of defects in China and the rising cost of manufacturing there.

Summary

- Yes, it is "who you know" that's most important. Develop excellent relationships with people and create a wide network of colleagues as you progress in your career. Keep in contact with colleagues at other companies by phone calls, emails, lunches, and social media.

- Also, it is "what you know" that's important. You should be competent in your work.

Questions to Ask Yourself

- How many people do you know well at work?

- How many people have you gone to lunch or coffee within the last year, month and week?

- How many people have you helped somehow in the last year?

- Does your manager's manager know and like you? Have you developed that relationship?

- Do people from other departments in your company know and like you?

- What else can you do in the next year to build your network of work relationships?

Additional Resources

- Forbes Magazine-"7 Books To Help You Improve Your Business Networking And Build Real Relationships"

- Chron.com-"mportance of Employee Performance in Business Organizations"

- Psychology Today-"It's Not What You Know. It's Who You Know. Whose fault is that?"

Chapter 9: People & Their Behaviors at Work

"The greatest ability in business is to get along with others and to influence their actions."

~ John Hancock

Lesson 23: People Create Problems

Here is what every manager knows: most of the problems with a project or work have to do with people. When something is wrong, it usually has to do with someone acting, saying or doing the wrong thing.

The politics of people at work can be exhausting, confusing and dangerous to one's career. If you don't understand what's going on and how you should respond to certain situations, you will be at a serious disadvantage.

Whether or not you want to participate in work politics, if you work with people, you are already in that environment.

This chapter talks about things you can do to succeed at work, regardless of politics.

Lesson 24: Be the Best Liked Programmer

Years ago at a large company, a student intern was working on a project. One day he lamented that although he was a Computer Science major, he thought he wasn't a great programmer. Maybe it was true, maybe not; what was important is that he felt that way.

His manager said "you don't have to be the best programmer. You only have to be the best liked programmer." Over the last 20 years, the former intern has had one successful position after another and now is in senior management at a major financial company.

This former intern is one of those people that others immediately like. He has a kind, relaxed personality, and a ready smile. He is smart, respectful of others and helpful to all. Obviously, his parents did a great job teaching him how to be a very likable person. Wouldn't it be wonderful if everyone was that gifted?

For many people, personal and professional relationships are difficult. It takes a while for people to get to know them. It can be a struggle. If you are one of these people, it can be frustrating to see how easily others get along.

You can improve your professional and personal relations by gaining new skills. One of the best sources is "Dale Carnegie's course on People Skills." In the 1930s, Carnegie wrote a book called "How to Win Friends and Influence People." This book has never been out of print and has been published for over 80 years (yes, they have updated it). It should be required reading for everyone in business.

Summary

- It is very important to be liked and respected at work. Working on your "likability" will only help your career.

- Everyone can improve their skills in human relations.

- The people you work with will only appreciate anything you do in this area–because it makes the experience better for them.

Questions to Ask Yourself

- Do I think I am likable? Do others think I am likable?

- Do people engage in conversation with me often, or try to avoid me?

- Who is the most likable person I know at work? Which of their skills and attributes do I admire?

- Which of their skills and attributes would I like to develop in myself?

Additional Resources

- Fortune Magazine – "Why It's Better to be Like Than to be Respected"

- Dale Carnegie course on People Skills – Highly recommended

- "How to Win Friends and Influence People." – Highly recommended

Lesson 25: Social Animals and Alcohol

People are social animals. They want to engage with others. It is part of our nature.

What is the best way to be social with people in the workplace? This has changed over the last 20 years. It used to be "let's go out for a drink after work." Now that's frowned on for several reasons, mostly because of the alcohol and drunk driving laws. There's also the variable that alcohol numbs normal inhibitions, making us more likely to say and do things we wouldn't typically do.

Try this once. If you go out for a drink, go out with several people and avoid drinking alcohol. Have soda or tonic water with a lime for a drink (it's will look like a cocktail). Then listen and watch as the next couple of hours proceed. What did you learn about the people you didn't know before? What effect did the alcohol have on them?

Avoiding alcohol is especially useful at company functions and annual parties. You will see people go nuts when there's an open bar and scarf down beer like its water. But not taking part will give you a distinct advantage. Use functions like this to watch people and observe behavior. Listen well, you will hear things you wouldn't otherwise hear; some of which may be insightful and useful.

Lesson 26: Safe Zones and People's Time

Going to lunch and meeting at coffee shops during the day are excellent and safe venues. It automatically removes the alcohol, and the atmosphere is lighter. You also will most likely not have to worry about awkward situations. Open break rooms and other public areas in a company are also good places to talk with people.

The important thing is just to be respectful of the other person's time. For example, you can go to someone's cubicle and talk for a while, but if they are working on an important or time-sensitive project, they might not appreciate it. They might not want to hurt your feelings by saying anything. So ask if they have time to socialize before you sit down in their office.

Lesson 27: What to Talk About

Talking with others is an opportunity to share a part of yourself. You can talk about work, mutual topics of interest, hobbies, weather, etc. But with social issues, politics or religion be very careful, especially if you don't really know the other people. Even if you know them, tread carefully. Once you say something, you can't take it back. And it is easy to create controversy over nothing. Even civil conversations about hot button topics seem to elicit only bad behavior and rancor, so just avoid it.

Avoid gossip and talking negatively about other people. This only creates problems and what you say may end up only hurting you.

Lesson 28: How You Dress

You should always "dress for success," as they say. Dressing for work shouldn't be difficult. Dress should always be conservative for both men and women. You know what that means: ironed shirts and pants for men, the same or dresses for women, showing no cleavage and skirts at or above the knees.

This clothing isn't acceptable: any clothing that makes other people uncomfortable. No leotards or body hose, no sweat pants or shirts, no shirts half opened, no t-shirts, shorts, flip-flops or anything else that you would wear around the house. You can wear whatever you want at the office. Just know people always judge you by what you wear at work.

Lesson 29: Setting Behavior Boundaries

This statement is for both men and women: treat people with respect, not as objects. Don't act like you're a teenager on a date. The workplace or meeting for lunch or coffee with coworkers is NOT the place to look for a mate, so just forget it. To do any less than this is to ignore the dignity of the other person and their hopes, dreams, and aspirations. Key point: never look at work for your next significant other.

Most people want to do a good day's work (and get paid for it), then go home and leave their company in their rearview mirror. They don't go to work for any other reason.

The "Me-Too" movement has raised the visibility and importance of treating all people with respect. So it is always best to act appropriately in the workplace.

Lesson 30: Language

Do not use profanity of any kind. It is never acceptable in any language. Remember, you are always being judged. Language is either a powerful tool for success or a liability that will cause you problems.

Also, if you and a friend speak any language other than English, always speak English in the workplace. It is annoying and impolite to speak another language around people that don't speak your language.

Lesson 31: Inspect, Don't Expect

"Nothing is what it seems," said a character in the series "Medici" on Netflix. There is wisdom in that statement.

To always know the truth you should inspect, not expect. Don't expect that something will ever be the way you think because often that will only disappoint you. Disappointment is bad enough, but if you decide based on an incorrect expectation, your decisions may also be flawed. However, if you inspect, you will know the truth of the matter 100% of the time. So inspect, don't expect.

Lesson 32: First Seek to Understand

It's always best to first seek to understand before you speak. Understand the who, what, where, when, and why, before you say or respond to anything. You need to ask the right questions and carefully listen to the answers. Then speak. When in doubt, listen more and speak less.

The concept of understanding first and then seek to be understood isn't new. The problem is that many people don't do this and therefore they make mistakes or say the wrong thing.

Lesson 33: Human Resources Real Purpose

Human Resources (HR) functions as a vital part of any company. However, it is important that you understand what HR is and what HR isn't.

The primary purpose of HR is to manage risk for the company. That risk is people that work at the company. HR publishes long guidelines for personal and corporate conduct. Their focus is on making employees work within all those policies and procedures.

The primary purpose of HR isn't to help employees. That's the truth. If you go to HR with a problem, chances are high they won't solve the problem. They will, however, contact your manager to solve it. Then HR will document the problem and resolution. So, be very careful when working with HR and talking with them about anything. They aren't your friends; they aren't there to make employee lives better. Their purpose is only to manage risk.

Also, most of the time, HR will support the manager over any employee, again because of the risk the employee may present to the company. This is because they see the manager as part of the company, but employees don't carry the same importance. Even if the employee is right, it rarely ends well for the employee once they contact HR. It makes the situation worse. The "Me Too" movement may impact how HR acts in the future. Time will tell.

Summary

- People are social animals and there are definite rules about what is and isn't acceptable conduct in the workplace.

- Coffee shops and restaurants during the day are safe zones.

- Avoid drinking alcohol in work social situations.

- Where possible avoid talking about hot button topics like social, political and religious issues

- People in the workplace are there to work. Treat everyone with respect and civility.

- Inspect, Don't Expect.

- Human Resources' main purpose is to control risk for the company.

Questions to Ask Yourself

- Have I been in situations at work where I felt awkward? If so, what could I do to avoid that?

- Am I sociable with people at work? If not, what are acceptable places to meet people near work?

- Do I dress appropriately for the professional workplace? If the president of the company was coming by my office tomorrow, would I dress the same way or differently?

- Have I ever talked about a subject at work that offended or angered other people? What did I learn from that experience? Was talking about that subject worth angering someone else?

- Do I have any unrealistic expectations of the people I work with? If so, are any of those non-work related?

- Do I assume a lot? Do I expect that things will be a certain way, only to find out that those things aren't correct?

Additional Resources

- Fast Company – "How To Deal With The 10 Most Uncomfortable Work Situations"

- TheBalanceCareers.com – "10 Tips for Dealing With Difficult People at Work"

- VeryWellMind.com – "Preparing for Small Talk: A List of the Best and Worst Topics"

- TheBalanceCareers.com – "Dress for Work Success: A Sample Business Casual Dress Code"

- TheWorkPlace.org – "HR is not there to be your friend. It's there to protect the company"

Chapter 10: Managing Your Manager

"After one look at this planet, any visitor from outer space would say 'I want to see the manager.'"

~ William S. Burroughs

Lesson 34: You Must Manage Your Manager

Everyone should manage the relationship they have with their manager. But many people just plod through work, without giving it a second thought. Managing your manager is essential to having an excellent relationship, establishing trust and building your career.

Did you think only your manager manages? Think again. Highly successful people manage their manager.

Lesson 35: No Surprises

No one likes to be surprised, but managers because of their occupation really HATE surprises. They have so many things to think about. Their job is juggling a dozen balls in the air at the same time. The last thing they want or need is for one of their employees to drop a "SURPRISE!" bomb on their desk.

A "SURPRISE" bomb may literally blow up your manager's day. It will be one more unexpected thing they have to deal with because you didn't or couldn't handle it. Is that something you really want to happen? How do you think your manager will react?

This is how to avoid surprising your manager:

- Set achievable expectations
- Warn them as soon as you can
- Make it easy for them
- Create a drama-free zone
- What you say you will do
- Be reliable and trustworthy
- Always make them look good
- With problems have solutions

Set Achievable Expectations

A previous section spoke of the importance of negotiating realistic and achievable goals and deadlines for projects and deliverables. This is especially true for managing your manager. If you need more time, don't wait until the last day to ask for another 2 weeks. Ask for that at the beginning of the project.

Not setting achievable expectations with your manager is one of the best ways to surprise them. Worse yet, they will trust you less and likely feel the need to watch over your work more closely.

If you set achievable expectations and accomplish those, how do you think your manager will feel about you?

Lesson 36: Warn Them as Soon as You Can

When you see trouble coming, let them know!

You have intuition, so you know when something doesn't seem right. It could be your little voice saying "I don't think this vendor will meet their deadline," it could be "at this rate I will blow our annual advertising budget in only 6 months." The point is, there are always signs when something will go wrong; whether that's 3 months or 3 days from now. Your job is to recognize those signs and do something about it!

You must warn your manager when you think anything negative could happen – this isn't "crying wolf." This is "raising the flag" and saying "we need to look at this to discern the risk, it's effect on the project and put into place preventative measures, if necessary." Also, it gives the manager time to think – you're not telling them at the last moment, so there's time to come up with a well thought out mitigation plan.

Such a conversation is also an opportunity to discuss fully the situation and develop trust. Your manager will know that you are warning them to protect them from a failure somewhere and they will appreciate it.

Lesson 37: Make it Easy for Them

Make interactions with your manager something pleasant and predictable so he can relax when he talks with you. For example, If you have a meeting with him and you want to talk about an email or several emails you sent him in the past week, have those emails printed out and with you for the meeting. Don't expect he will remember your email or know where it is.

What could I do to make things easier for my manager this week?

Lesson 38: Create a Drama-Free Zone

Consider the experience of traveling by plane: There is packing your bags, getting ready for the trip, getting to the airport, checking in bags, worry about others (if you have kids with you), getting your boarding pass, getting through the TSA checkpoint, walking to the gate, waiting, walking to another gate (if the gate changed), watching out for strangers and thieves, boarding the plane and arranging your carry-on bags. Then you sit down. Do you remember the relief you felt when you finally sat down after all that effort?

A manager's day is like traveling by plane every day. There are dozens of things to worry about and many complex steps. Only when the day is over can managers relax and rest (and that's only if they shut off their phone and PC). Unless you create a drama-free zone. Then your manager can relax at that meeting.

Managers often call the job of managing both "the best of all possible worlds" and "proof that no good deed goes unpunished." This is because people act like children in kindergarten. There is whining, arguments, people missing deadlines, people upsetting clients, absences without cause, those employees taking 2-hour lunches, those missing key meetings, sub-quality work product, etc., etc., etc.

Drama-free zone means you are the adult in the room. It means your behavior is the same every day–no whining, no surprises, no issues, no problems, no drama. Your meeting with them may be the only easy, drama-free meeting they have all week. You become for them an ally they can trust; one less person they have to worry about.

Lesson 39: What You Say You Will Do

Do what you say you will do. When you make a commitment with your manager, honor that commitment. If you say you will be in at 7 A.M. on Saturday to get the packages ready for 10 A.M. shipment for a trade show next Monday, you had better be there at 7 A.M. Showing up at 8 A.M. won't earn you any trust points. Especially, if you find that your manager came in and finished your work.

If you aren't acting and building this kind of trust and expectation with your manager, eventually you may regret it.

Lesson 40: Be Reliable and Trustworthy

Nothing says you like and respect your manager as much as being reliable and trustworthy and doing that consistently over a proven period. That is the gold standard everyone should work towards. If you aren't doing that, reconsider whether you really want to do that job.

The alternative to being reliable and trustworthy is that you become a liability or a negative variable for the manager. Liabilities and variables are mitigated or removed. Questions?

Lesson 41: Always Make Them Look Good

Always strive to make your manager look good. They can't be everywhere all the time and you are their representative when they aren't there. If you think you only represent yourself anytime you do something, think again. You work for someone and that person is accountable for you. If you do something wrong, they get the call, not you. They become the one that has to handle "something."

When you don't see your manager, it is because she is earnestly working on something–she may even hide out in a different part of the building to get work done. There is no other reason managers are absent from view.

If your manager creates a project for you to do and it turns out well, give them their due credit for their role in the project-praise them directly. They never get that kind of praise from employees, so they will appreciate it. Just to clarify, I am not talking about brown-nosing; I am talking about only sincere, deserved praise.

You may find this shocking, but managers are only people–just like you and me. Managers are far from perfect. Occasionally they will forget things, fail at something, remember something wrong. When this happens, don't be the one that sits silent or puts them on the spot. Be the person who asks this question "What can I do to help you resolve this?" Managers can and will fall short, like everyone else.

The last time you fell short of a goal, what did your manager say to you?

Lesson 42: With Problems Have Solutions

When you go to your manager with a problem or roadblock, have a list of solutions. Don't expect that your manager will just solve it for you. Only children expect their parents to make everything all right.

Manager's need problem solvers, because the world and work is full of problems. So, while one of their jobs is to "remove roadblocks" from your path, it isn't true they have to figure out the best solution. You are the subject expert of whatever is going on; your manager may know nothing about it.

Once you have identified that you have a problem that requires your manager's input or help, spend time to develop different scenarios that can solve the problem. Chart out on paper or slides the problem and solutions. Then go to your manager and say "I have a problem that needs your review and input. Would you be able to look at what I have prepared for possible solutions?" It will thrill your manager to do this because again, most people won't bother.

Summary

There are rules for managing your manager. These include:

- Never surprise your manager

- Always warn them when you see trouble coming

- Operate in a drama free zone and share that with your manager

- Be the adult in the room, not the child

- Always make your manager look good

- When you have a problem, go to them with solutions

Questions to Ask Yourself

- The last time I surprised a manager, what was their reaction? What were the consequences for me?

- Have I seen trouble coming in the past and not recognized it? If so why? What was the outcome afterward?

- Do I work in a drama free zone or do I create a drama zone? If I create drama why? What do I get out of it? Is my work life better or worse for it?

- Am I the child or the adult in the room? If I am the child why? What do I get out of being the child? Does that make me happy somehow?

- The last time I went to a manager with a problem, did I also bring solutions? If not, why not? Did I think he or she could solve all my problems? What was the result? How did I feel afterward?

Additional Resources

- Forbes Magazine – "12 Easy Ways To Manage Your Boss"

- TheMuse.com – "How to Deal With the 5 Most Negative Types of Co-workers"

- Inc.com – "10 Ways to Cut Workplace Drama and Make Work Fun Again"

- TheMuse.com – "5 Ways to Make Your Boss Look Good—and Get Ahead in the Process"

- Forbes Magazine – "Don't Bring Problems To Your Manager-Bring Solutions"

If you like this book and find it useful, use a pencil and add your own notes to it. That way you'll be able to refer to previously read topics more easily in the future.

Chapter Bonus: Long Term Success

"It takes 20 years to build a reputation and five minutes to ruin it. If you think about that, you'll do things differently."

~ Warren Buffett

Lesson 43: Build Your Brand and Reputation

If you want a strong career, what you really are saying is that "you want to be a strong brand."

Brands are all around us: food, electronics, cars, even the town we live in can be considered a brand. You know immediately which brands you can trust and which you can't. It is the same for people. People with outstanding brands are the ones you go to for help, the ones you befriend, the ones you want to work with, and the ones you want to speak at your professional association's meeting.

So how do you develop your own professional brand?

Your Brand is Everything

First, you need to understand that everyone is always judging you: your attitude, your dress, the things you say and how you say those and what you do. Judgments are the rule, not the exception in the workplace.

Previous chapters spoke about people, politics and the workplace. Here is where the rubber hits the road: your perceived brand worth. Look over the previous chapters again and think about what you can do this year to improve your brand perception.

Lesson 44: Build a Work Record and Chronology

One way to build your personal brand is by having a work history that makes sense. It doesn't have to be perfect. It doesn't have to be longer than 10 years. However, it should be a career that will be understandable to anyone that reads your resume or looks at your LinkedIn profile.

For example, if you start as a software developer, then a few years later become a senior software developer and a few years after that you become software architect, you have an easy-to-understand work record and chronology.

If you jump around from one job focus to another, it will take an explanation for other people to understand. It doesn't mean that it's not good experience; it means that you will need to pull it together in a coherent way. The narrative must make sense to the reader.

Lesson 45: Keep Track of Your Accomplishments

After you complete a project or a large accomplishment, record key information about it. The reason you want to do this is so you don't forget. This information can someday in your resume, or used as a success story in an interview. What you are creating is a work journal and work archive.

This should be a simple task as you will have just completed something. Record details in an MS Word document (The worksheets are available at coachyourselfbooks.com/worksheets/):

- The problem or focus of the project

- Your role (position)

- What you did

- The result

- Mention any relevant numbers. For example "saved X number of dollars," "completed in 9 months instead of 12," "managed X number of people," "budget of $X,".

- Quantify the success from your manager's perspective:

- Why this was important

- Who benefited from it

- How did this add to the organization's success

- Completion Date

- Project Duration

Keep one folder on your work computer and one folder on your home computer. It is paramount that you always have all information in 2 different places on 2 different computer systems. That is the only true way to avoid losing work.

- Title the filename with this information:
- Name of project: System Migration of X
- Your role on the project: Technical Writer
- What you did: Wrote User Guide
- Date of Project: 02-22-2018

If you follow that format, the filename will look something like this: SSysMigX-TechWriter-WroteUserGuide-02152018.docx

Now you have it written in an MS Word document for when you need it. Print that to a PDF and put both files in the folder titled "Work-Accomplishments." You can separate it by role or year. Or you can just lump it into one large folder. What matters is that you can find it when you need to find it. Otherwise, it's useless.

Also, put the actual work product, in this case, the user guide, in a separate folder titled "Work-Samples." Add the same date (as the accomplishment) to the end of the current filename. For example, UserGuide.docx becomes UserGuide-02152018. docx. Also, print this file to a PDF, so you have a copy that will always be readable and accessible, regardless of what happens to software and technology.

At completion, you will have 4 files:

- The accomplishment description: SysMigX-TechWriter-WroteUserGuide-02152018.docx

- The accomplishment description in PDF format: SysMigX-TechWriter-WroteUserGuide-02152018.pdf

- The finished work product: UserGuide-02152018.docx

- A PDF copy of the work product: UserGuide-02152018.pdf

Keeping a record of accomplishments, the details and the work product will build an accurate history for you to refer to throughout your career. If you do this consistently, you will never be at a loss to talk about yourself or your accomplishments.

Lesson 46: Create and Maintain a Portfolio

A portfolio is a showcase of your best work. You can share this with your employer at end of the year reviews and with future employers when interviewing. Visual aids in almost any professional setting are powerful and persuasive.

If you have done the previous step (keeping track of your accomplishments), building a portfolio will be a simple process. Look over your archive of work and select the best of each type of work that's relevant.

What is relevant for your end of the year review will be the work you completed in the past year. What is relevant for a job interview will be whatever work samples best fit the job description. For example, if you are applying for a Marketing Manager job, showing examples of marketing brochures and advertising campaigns would be relevant.

You can provide these in a variety of formats. You can:

- Load the description and work product for each project on a flash drive

- Have it on a laptop or tablet you bring with you

- Print it out and put it in clear plastic sleeves in a loose-leaf notebook

- Put it on a site like Wix or a website with your own domain name

The portfolio must be easy to get to so your audience can see it when necessary.

Lesson 47: Create and Update Your Resume

Your resume should always be up to date. If you aren't doing this yet, you might work on it today. Most people leave their resume alone until they need it (like when they leave a job unexpectedly and have to find another). This is the wrong time to update your resume.

Why?

If you do a good job, others will notice. Some may ask you for your resume even if you aren't looking for a job. If your resume isn't up to date, what will you do? You've just lost a job, do you really think you'll in the best frame of mind to update your resume?

Lesson 48: Build Your Network

Throughout your career, you must build and grow your professional network. Your work alone will never be enough to get you noticed or to find the next job.

There are two ways to build your network: online and offline.

You don't have to be an online influencer to build out your digital footprint online. You need the interest, a plan, and some work.

Online you should use LinkedIn.com:

- If you don't have a profile already, create one on LinkedIn.

- Expand your network and link to as many people as you can. You need not know these people well to link with them. The important thing is building out a vast audience you can share things with.

- Write posts and articles about subjects you feel passionate about-especially in your profession.

- Always be positive. On LinkedIn.com, anything negative or taking positions on social, political or religious subjects won't get read. If those get read, they won't get forwarded to others. What you want to do is start a conversation with others and have that conversation multiply into many "likes" and "shares."

- Remember that online, like face to face, you will always be judged. Be interesting, positive, polite and helpful.

- Join LinkedIn groups that interest you, are career relevant, and you can contribute to.

- Follow influencers you admire or that interest you.

- Like and re-post things you see that might interest others.

Other Online Networking use:

- Email,

- Text Messaging

- Any other Social Media you like

- to stay in touch with others at least once a month.

Offline:

- Use the telephone to call people you have worked with to stay in touch.

- Go to networking events when you see those available

- Go to lunch with colleagues you want to deepen the relationship with

- When there are events at work, participate! Don't just grab food and go back to your cube—no one will see you!

- Become socially engaged at work events for the betterment of others is a win-win for good networking.

- Charities are a great way to pay it forward and meet like-minded people. Some companies do projects several times a year for "Habitat for Humanity." There are literally thousands of charities out there that need volunteers.

- If you go to church, consider taking part in one of their social groups

Look at it this way: each time you meet someone is an opportunity. It's not a coincidence or a chance encounter, there's a purpose. It's up to you to figure out what that purpose is. It could be cheerful communication with another human being.

Likewise, they might be the next person you work for in your career.

Summary

- It is very important that you build both a brand and a reputation in your chosen profession.

- You can do this by:

- Building a good work record and chronology

- Keeping track of your accomplishments

- Creating and maintaining a portfolio of your best work

- Creating and maintaining your resume

- Building your professional network both online and offline

- Keep that network alive by contacting people often

Questions to Ask Yourself

- When I look at my resume, does the career progression make sense (tell a coherent story)?

- Do I have a good and easy way to track my accomplishments? If not, why not?

- Do I have a portfolio? If not, why not?

- Have I ever seen anyone create and use a portfolio? If yes, what was the response of the audience when they viewed it?

- What have I done this week, month and year to build and feed my professional network?

- What could I do today to reach out to someone new at my workplace?

Additional Resources

- Forbes.com – "8 Reasons a Powerful Personal Brand Will Make You Successful"

- QuickSprout.com – "The Complete Guide to Building Your Personal Brand"

- TopResume.com – "How to Track Your Work Accomplishments Throughout the Year"

- WikiHow.com – "How to Create a Career Portfolio"

- TopResume.com – "Update Your Outdated Resume: The 7-Step Modern Resume"

- GoodCall.com – "Making Connections: How to Create and Cultivate Your Professional Network"

- BusinessInsider.com – "7 Way to Master Online Networking"

Thank you for reading this book

I hope this book has been helpful to you. If you liked it, please share it with others who could benefit from it. I wish you all the best in your future life and career. If you'd like to reach out to me, use the contact form on my website.

Please Don't Forget

Don't forget to download your free:

- Collection of forms

- List of all online resources with hyperlinks

The worksheets are available at:
coachyourselfbooks.com/worksheets/

Consider Writing a Review of this Book

If you have enjoyed this book and found it helpful, please consider writing a review on Amazon. It will help others find it too. Thank you.

https://www.amazon.com/dp/1091977135